High-Stakes Careers

CRISIS NEGOTIATORS

Abby Doty

WWW.APEXEDITIONS.COM

Copyright © 2026 by Apex Editions, Mendota Heights, MN 55120. All rights reserved. No part of this book may be reproduced or utilized in any form or by any means without written permission from the publisher.

Apex is distributed by North Star Editions:
sales@northstareditions.com | 888-417-0195

Produced for Apex by Red Line Editorial.

Photographs ©: iStockphoto, cover, 1, 4–5, 12–13, 14–15, 16–17, 28–29, 32–33, 44–45, 58; Shutterstock Images, 6–7, 8–9, 18–19, 30–31, 40–41, 50–51, 54–55; Santi Visalli Inc./Archive Photos/Getty Images, 10–11; Romeo Gacad/AFP/Getty Images, 20–21; Adam Butler/AP Images, 22–23; Christian Escobar Mora/AP Images, 24–25; Mike Fiala/AFP/Getty Images, 26–27; Randy Squires/AP Images, 34–35; Jessica Rinaldi/The Boston Globe/Getty Images, 36–37; Gregory Smith/Corbis Historical/Getty Images, 39; Noel Celis/AFP/Getty Images, 42–43; Guillermo Arias/AP Images, 46–47; Bernard Bisson/Sygma/Getty Images, 49; Master Sgt. Ashlee J. L. Sherrill/Minnesota National Guard/AB Forces News Collection/Alamy, 53; Lucas Barioulet/AFP/Getty Images, 56–57

Library of Congress Control Number: 2025930332

ISBN
979-8-89250-667-0 (hardcover)
979-8-89250-701-1 (ebook pdf)
979-8-89250-685-4 (hosted ebook)

Printed in the United States of America
Mankato, MN
082025

NOTE TO PARENTS AND EDUCATORS

Apex books are designed to build literacy skills in striving readers. Exciting, high-interest content attracts and holds readers' attention. The text is carefully leveled to allow students to achieve success quickly.

TABLE OF CONTENTS

Chapter 1
SAVING HOSTAGES 5

Chapter 2
NEGOTIATING A CRISIS 9

Chapter 3
HOSTAGE TAKERS 18

Chapter 4
OTHER CRISES 28

Story Spotlight
WACO, TEXAS 38

Chapter 5
RISKS AND CHALLENGES 41

Story Spotlight
TERRY WAITE 48

Chapter 6
TYPES OF TRAINING 50

SKILLS CHECKLIST • 59
COMPREHENSION QUESTIONS • 60
GLOSSARY • 62
TO LEARN MORE • 63
ABOUT THE AUTHOR • 63
INDEX • 64

In 1993, robbers targeted a Chase bank. This company has many locations throughout New York City.

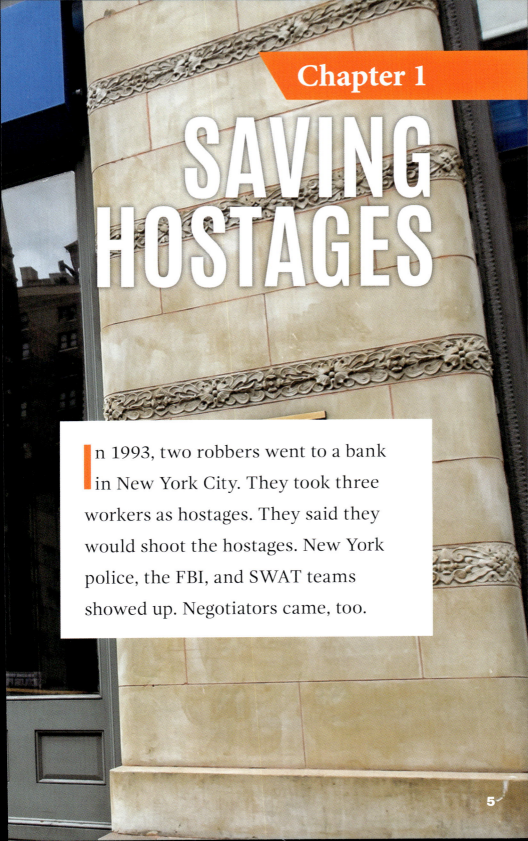

Chapter 1

SAVING HOSTAGES

In 1993, two robbers went to a bank in New York City. They took three workers as hostages. They said they would shoot the hostages. New York police, the FBI, and SWAT teams showed up. Negotiators came, too.

Negotiators often speak on the phone. That way, hostage takers cannot see them.

Negotiators spoke with the robbers over the phone. They talked for more than six hours. The negotiators listened closely. They gained the robbers' trust. They convinced the robbers to give up. The robbers let the hostages go. Then the robbers came out, too. The negotiators helped save the day.

FINDING A VOICE

Talks during a negotiation can get tense. Negotiators use their voices to help. They may make their voices deep and slow. This makes them sound in charge. It helps them get people to do what they ask.

Police may rush to the spot where shots are fired.

Chapter 2
NEGOTIATING A CRISIS

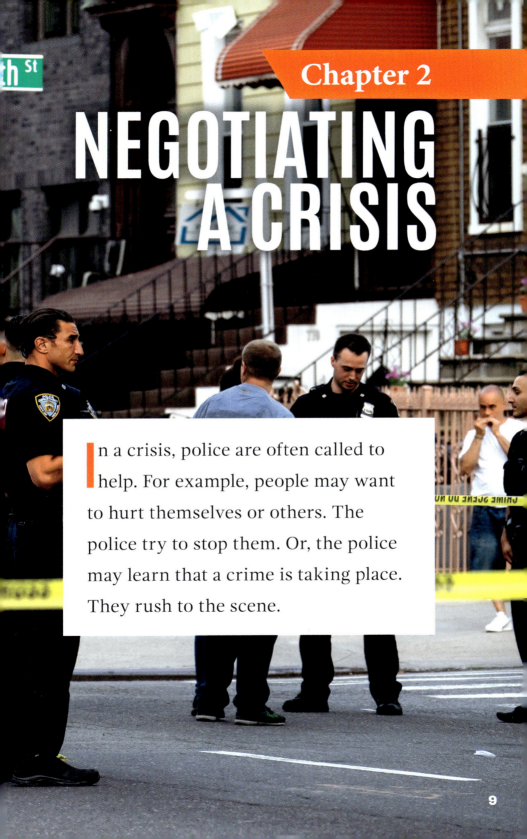

In a crisis, police are often called to help. For example, people may want to hurt themselves or others. The police try to stop them. Or, the police may learn that a crime is taking place. They rush to the scene.

In the past, police at crime scenes just told suspects to surrender. But some suspects did not. So, the police would attack. However, attacking was risky. People could be hurt or killed.

In the 1970s, police created negotiation teams. These teams try to convince suspects to give up peacefully. Teams also talk with people who threaten to hurt themselves or others. They try to get these people to change their minds.

FIRST TEAM

In 1971, prisoners took over a prison in New York. They held 42 workers hostage. Police attacked. The fight killed 33 inmates. Ten prison workers also died. Afterward, the New York police created the first negotiation team.

Fighting between police and prisoners at Attica State Prison in New York caused massive damage. People called for more peaceful solutions.

In many of these cases, people want to keep the police away. These people may hide in buildings. They may refuse to come out.

Negotiators might speak to people over the phone. Or they might use bullhorns. Whatever the method, they try to start talking as soon as possible. They work to calm people down. They try to keep people from hurting anyone.

A bullhorn makes a person's voice louder so they can be heard from farther away.

Negotiators often work alongside SWAT teams. SWAT teams are trained to work in risky situations. They can search buildings and capture people. If needed, they use weapons to take down suspects. Negotiators try to convince suspects to surrender first. But they don't always succeed. SWAT teams may then step in.

SNEAK ATTACK

In 1980, six men with guns took over a building in London. They held 26 people hostage. Negotiators talked with the terrorists for days. They convinced them to release a few hostages. But one hostage was killed. So, British troops attacked. They sneaked into the building and took the terrorists down.

SWAT teams may use weapons if negotiations fail.

Like the police, FBI agents work to solve and prevent crimes.

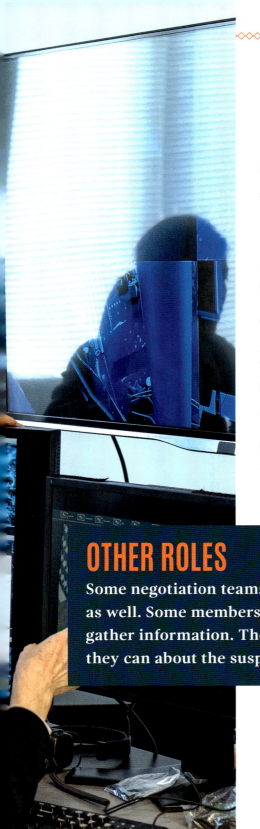

Negotiators work in teams. Some are part of police forces. Others work for the FBI.

Many teams have one main negotiator. This person speaks with the suspect or person in crisis. A second negotiator focuses on talking with other police officers or FBI agents.

OTHER ROLES

Some negotiation teams have other members as well. Some members take notes. Others gather information. They learn as much as they can about the suspects or hostages.

Chapter 3
HOSTAGE TAKERS

Some negotiations involve hostages. Hostage takers usually want something. Some ask for money. Some want governments or police to do things. They may threaten to hurt hostages if their demands are not met. But if they get what they want, they may let the hostages go.

Hostages are often tied up or trapped inside buildings.

Negotiators listen to the demands. They try to learn what hostage takers are thinking and planning. They also work to calm down the hostage takers. That way, hostages are less likely to get hurt.

PLAN OR NO PLAN

Some people plan in advance to take hostages. Often, they have a political goal. For example, they may ask a country to release prisoners. Other people don't plan to take hostages. They just want to protect themselves from police. So, they take nearby people captive.

In 2007, a man held people hostage in a court room in the Philippines. He tried to escape out a window.

Next, negotiators build rapport. They try to get hostage takers to trust them. They want the hostage takers to feel heard. This makes it easier for negotiators to persuade them to do things.

In February 2000, hostage takers took over a plane. Negotiators convinced them to let the passengers go.

BROKEN TRUST

Negotiators must pay careful attention. If they forget something or get a detail wrong, trust can break. Hostage takers may feel like the negotiators are not really listening.

Often, negotiators focus on the demands. They may agree to some of what hostage takers ask for. For example, they may send food. Negotiators often persuade hostage takers to change other demands. Or they ask for things in return. They may ask for the release of some hostages. Or they may ask to see hostages. This shows they are still alive.

PROOF OF LIFE

Hostage takers may claim that hostages are alive or unharmed. But they could be lying. To find out, negotiators may ask for proof. Hostage takers may send photos or videos. Or negotiators may talk to hostages on the phone.

Fighters in Colombia took many people hostage in the early 2000s. Some were released. They brought photos of others who were still held hostage.

As they are talking, negotiators try to sound friendly and calm. They keep their voices low and even. They try not to argue. They don't want to anger the hostage takers.

Negotiators may also stall. For example, they may ask lots of questions. They try to keep hostage takers talking as long as possible. This gives police more time to plan. It also makes reaching a peaceful ending more likely.

In 2000, a young man held about 30 kids hostage at a school. Police convinced him to let them go. The kids were reunited with their parents.

Chapter 4
OTHER CRISES

In other crises, people put themselves in danger. They may go somewhere high up. Or they may lock themselves in buildings. They may try to hurt themselves. Negotiators work to convince them not to.

Police may be called to help if people seem likely to jump from bridges or buildings.

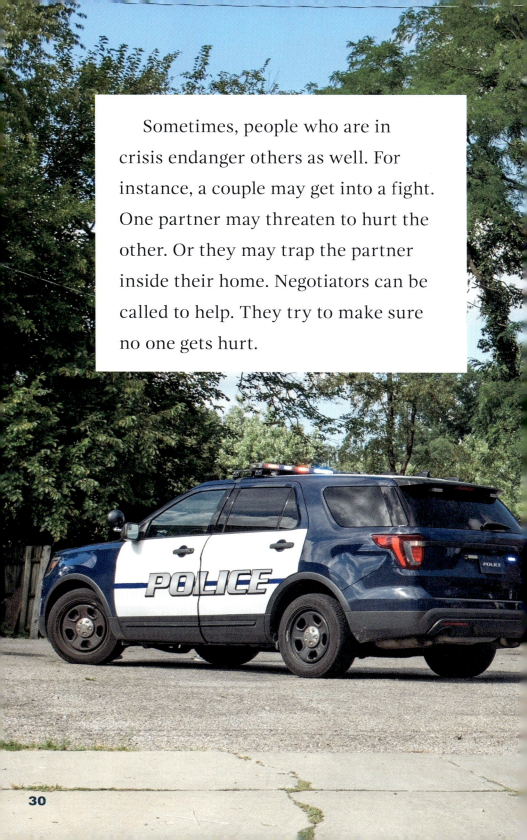

Sometimes, people who are in crisis endanger others as well. For instance, a couple may get into a fight. One partner may threaten to hurt the other. Or they may trap the partner inside their home. Negotiators can be called to help. They try to make sure no one gets hurt.

Police are often called to help stop fights.

If people are a danger to themselves or others, their emotions run high. Emotional people do not always think things through. They may act suddenly. Or they may become violent. So, negotiators work to keep everyone calm. They try to show they are there to help.

ACTIVE LISTENING

Many negotiators use active listening. This is a way of paying careful attention. The negotiators ask questions. They may repeat back what a person says. This helps show they understand.

Negotiators help people in crisis stay safe.

Some people in crisis do not want help. They may tell police to go away. They may think police don't care about them.

Negotiators try to show that they do care. They show empathy for what people are going through. When people feel understood, they are less likely to hurt themselves or others.

REFUSING TO LEAVE

In 1997, police came to Shirley Allen's home. Her mental health was not good. The police tried to bring her somewhere for treatment. But Allen shut herself inside her home with a shotgun. She stayed there for 39 days. Police eventually brought her in.

Shirley Allen's family felt worried about her health, so they called the police.

In 2017, a man brought an axe to a radio station. Negotiators spoke with him and took him to a hospital.

Negotiators try to keep people from becoming more upset. They use talking to do this. They may focus on things the person likes or cares about. For example, a person may have a pet. Talking about this pet may make the person less angry. They may decide to give up peacefully.

MENTAL HEALTH

Mental health often plays a role in crisis situations. People may be unwell. So, mental health workers can be involved, too. They may answer questions about a person's condition. And they may give negotiators advice about what to say.

Story Spotlight

WACO, TEXAS

In February 1993, federal agents went to Waco, Texas. They tried to arrest David Koresh. He led a religious group called the Branch Davidians. The group and the agents fought one another. Then the group members hid inside their compound.

Negotiators spoke with the group for 51 days. They tried to get people to come out or let them in. Thirty-five people did leave. Then federal agents decided to attack. They used tanks and tear gas. Fire burned the compound. More than 75 people died.

The Branch Davidians' compound completely burned up when federal agents attacked.

Many people work part-time as negotiators. They also do other police work.

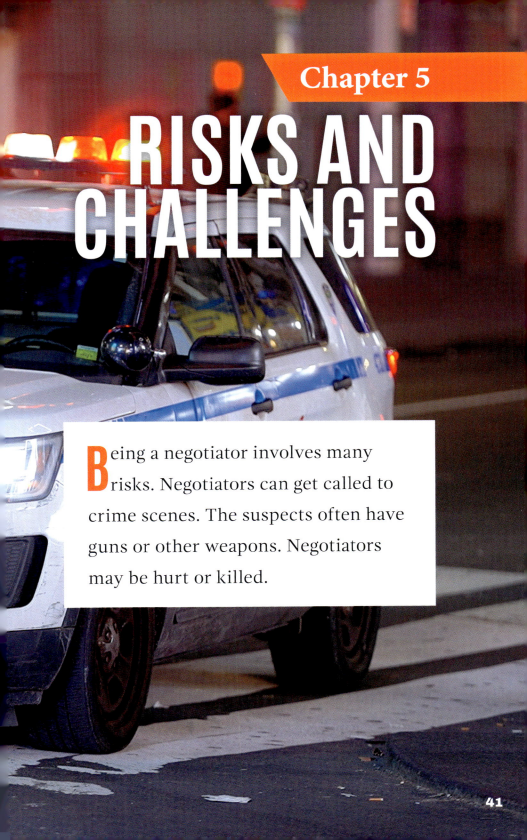

Chapter 5
RISKS AND CHALLENGES

Being a negotiator involves many risks. Negotiators can get called to crime scenes. The suspects often have guns or other weapons. Negotiators may be hurt or killed.

Talking with suspects is dangerous, too. Usually, negotiators stay hidden. They speak over the phone. Or they shout from far away. But sometimes, negotiators must get up close. That gives suspects a chance to hurt them. If negotiators approach, they move slowly and carefully. They try not to make people more upset.

In 2010, a man held people hostage on a bus in the Philippines. Negotiators walked up to talk with him.

Negotiators aren't the only ones in danger. If a negotiation goes badly, people can become violent. They might hurt themselves. Or they might harm hostages. If talking fails, fighting may break out. Police officers could be hurt. So could nearby people. Or suspects might get away. That would put more people in danger.

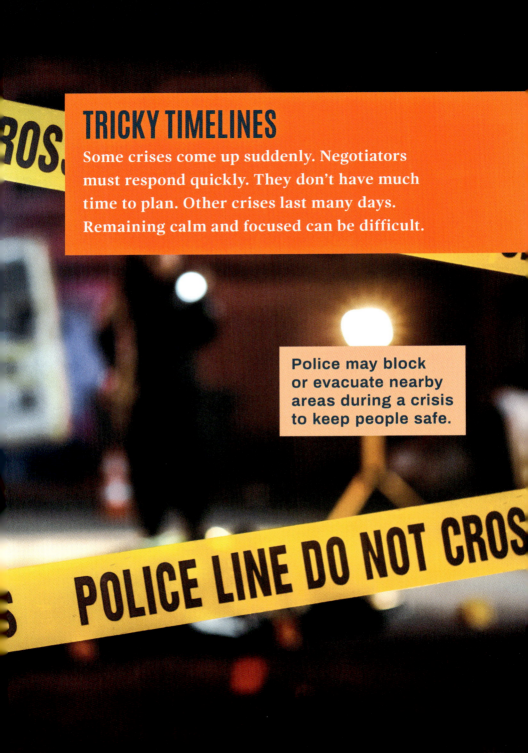

TRICKY TIMELINES

Some crises come up suddenly. Negotiators must respond quickly. They don't have much time to plan. Other crises last many days. Remaining calm and focused can be difficult.

Police may block or evacuate nearby areas during a crisis to keep people safe.

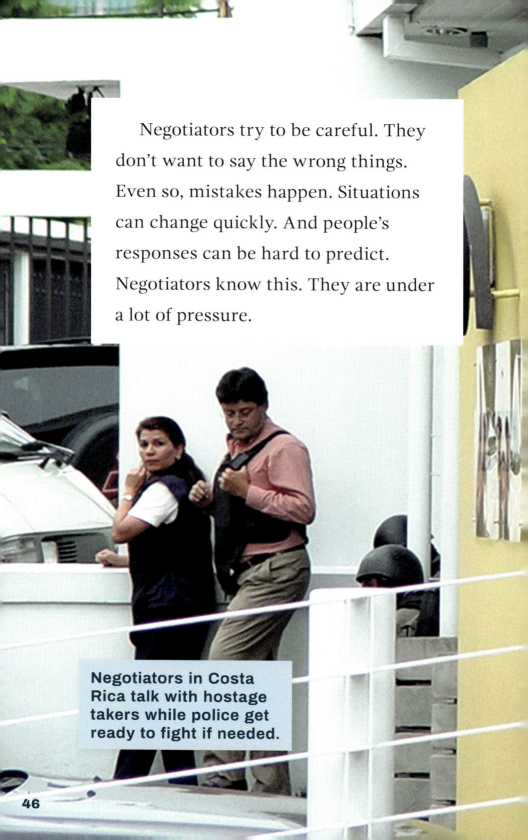

Negotiators try to be careful. They don't want to say the wrong things. Even so, mistakes happen. Situations can change quickly. And people's responses can be hard to predict. Negotiators know this. They are under a lot of pressure.

Negotiators in Costa Rica talk with hostage takers while police get ready to fight if needed.

FINDING THE TRUTH

Some suspects try to confuse negotiators. They may lie about who is in charge. Or they may not tell the truth about how many people are with them. As they talk, negotiators try to get as much information as possible. Then, they sort out what is true.

Story Spotlight

TERRY WAITE

Terry Waite is a British man who worked as a negotiator. In January 1987, he traveled to Beirut, Lebanon. He planned to speak with a religious group. This group had six hostages. Waite went to meet the hostage takers alone. They kidnapped him.

The group held Waite hostage for nearly five years. For much of that time, Waite was kept in a cell alone. His captors beat him. They also chained him to a wall. Government workers tried to get him released. He finally came home in November 1991.

> Terry Waite helped get several groups of hostages released. But in 1987, he became a hostage himself.

Chapter 6
TYPES OF TRAINING

Most people become negotiators after working as police officers. So, they must go through police training. This training usually takes several months. People learn about laws, patrols, and catching criminals. They train to fight and use guns.

By the time police officers finish training, they know skills to deal with many types of crises.

After training, police officers build experience. They work for a few years. They get practice dealing with crises. Then, they go through negotiation training. That often lasts a couple weeks.

Training explains the steps of the negotiating process. Officers learn what to do at each stage. They also talk through possible problems and how to solve them.

Training often describes different types of crises. Officers learn how to prepare for each one. For example, they study what to do if people seem likely to hurt themselves.

POLICE DEGREES

Some people go to college before joining police forces. They may get degrees in criminal justice. Or they may study psychology. That helps them understand how people think and act.

People in the military can also train as negotiators.

Training also teaches officers how to talk someone out of violence. It explains what to do if someone is angry. Officers practice ways to slow down and stay calm.

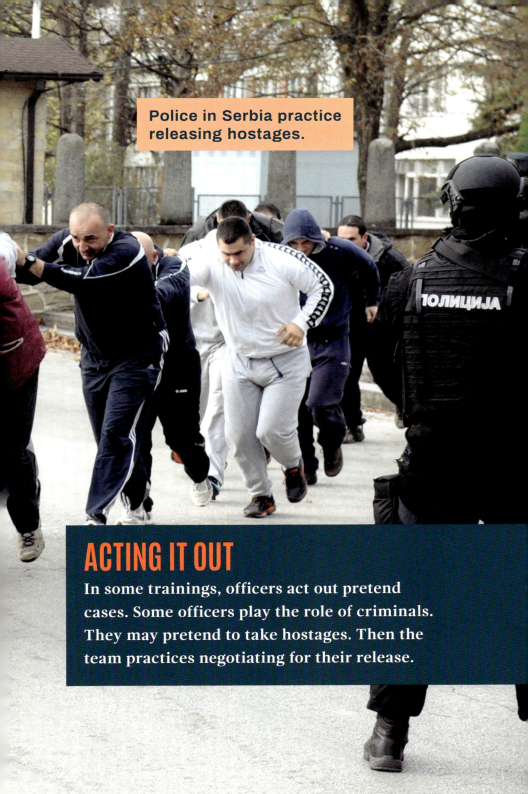

Police in Serbia practice releasing hostages.

ACTING IT OUT

In some trainings, officers act out pretend cases. Some officers play the role of criminals. They may pretend to take hostages. Then the team practices negotiating for their release.

Negotiators may also do more specific training. For example, they may learn how to lead teams. Or they may train to talk with people who are mentally unwell. All these skills help them work to end crises peacefully.

ALWAYS LEARNING
Training doesn't stop when negotiators get jobs. Some negotiators take classes to learn about mental health. Others meet together. They share and practice their skills. That helps them prepare for real cases.

A negotiator on the French police force trains in 2021.

✓ SKILLS CHECKLIST

- Communicating clearly

- Creating compromises and agreements

- Listening carefully and actively

- Staying calm even if others are angry

- Thinking quickly under pressure

- Understanding how other people think and feel

COMPREHENSION QUESTIONS

Write your answers on a separate piece of paper.

1. Write a paragraph that explains the main ideas in Chapter 3.

2. Would you want to work as a crisis negotiator? Why or why not?

3. When did police create crisis negotiation teams?
    - A. 1970s
    - B. 1980s
    - C. 1990s

4. Why would negotiators try to get the people they speak with to slow down?
    - A. so people have more time to think before acting
    - B. because acting quickly is never a good idea
    - C. because slowing down puts hostages at risk

5. What does **violent** mean in this book?

   *If a negotiation goes badly, people can become **violent**. They might hurt themselves. Or they might harm hostages.*

       A. staying calm
       B. acting friendly
       C. lashing out

6. What does **experience** mean in this book?

   *After training, police officers build **experience**. They work for a few years. They get practice dealing with crises.*

       A. facts learned by reading a book
       B. skills gained by doing something
       C. skills used only in class

Answer key on page 64.

GLOSSARY

criminal justice
The study of laws and crimes.

crisis
A time of great danger or serious problems.

empathy
The ability to understand how someone is feeling.

federal
Part of the top level of the US government, which involves the whole country.

hostages
People held as prisoners so that someone's demands will be met.

mental health
How well or unwell someone's mind is, including their emotions and thinking.

patrols
Paths people follow through an area to keep it safe and watch for problems.

psychology
The study of the mind and how it works.

rapport
A connection between people, often one that is close or friendly.

suspects
People the police think may be guilty of a crime.

terrorists
People who attack and scare others to reach their goals.

TO LEARN MORE

BOOKS

Campbell, Grace. *Crime Scene Investigators*. Lerner Publishing Group, 2021.

Dolbear, Emily. *Police Officers on the Scene*. The Child's World, 2022.

Hamilton, John. *FBI*. Abdo Publishing, 2022.

ONLINE RESOURCES

Visit **www.apexeditions.com** to find links and resources related to this title.

ABOUT THE AUTHOR

Abby Doty is a writer, editor, and booklover from Minnesota.

INDEX

active listening, 32
Allen, Shirley, 34

Branch Davidians, 38
bullhorns, 12

demands, 18, 20, 24

emotions, 32
empathy, 34

FBI, 5, 17

hostages, 5, 7, 10, 14, 17, 18, 20, 24–25, 44, 48, 55
hostage takers, 18, 20, 22–23, 24–26, 48

Koresh, David, 38

mental health, 34, 37, 56
mistakes, 46

phones, 7, 12, 25, 42
police, 5, 9–10, 12, 17, 18, 20, 26, 34, 44, 50, 52

questions, 26, 32, 37

release, 14, 20, 24, 48, 55

suspects, 10, 14, 17, 41–42, 44, 47
SWAT teams, 5, 14

training, 50, 52, 54–56

voices, 7, 26

Waite, Terry, 48

ANSWER KEY:

1. Answers will vary; 2. Answers will vary; 3. A; 4. A; 5. C; 6. B